AF497685

WASHINGTON IRVING

Travels in Missouri and the South

Reprint From the
MISSOURI HISTORICAL REVIEW,
October, 1910

NOTES BY F. A. SAMPSON

COLUMBIA, MISSOURI,
1910

WASHINGTON IRVING.

TRAVELS IN MISSOURI AND THE SOUTH.

Notes by F. A. Sampson.

In "Astoria" Washington Irving describes the expedition by land from St. Louis to the Pacific Coast, undertaken by the American Fur Company of which John Jacob Astor was the leading member, which expedition was organized in St. Louis in 1810. Of St. Louis the author says: (1)

"It possessed a motely population, composed of the Creole descendants of the original French colonists; the keen traders from the Atlantic States; the backwoodsmen of Kentucky and Tennessee; the Indian and half-breeds of the prairies; together with a singular aquatic race, that had grown up from the navigation of the rivers—the 'boatmen of the Mississippi'; who possessed habits, manners and almost a language, peculiarly their own, and strongly technical. They, at that time, were extremely numerous, and conducted the chief navigation and commerce of the Ohio and Mississippi, as the voyageurs did of the Canadian waters; but, like them, their consequence and characteristics are rapidly vanishing before the all-pervading intrusion of steamboats.

"The old French houses engaged in the Indian trade had gathered round them a train of dependents, mongrel Indians, and mongrel Frenchmen, who had intermarried with Indians. These they employed in their various expeditions by land and water. Various individuals of other countries had, of late years, pushed the trade further into the interior, to the upper waters of the Missouri, and had swelled the number of these hangers-on. Several of these traders had, two or three years

---

1. Astoria or anecdotes of an enterprise beyond the Rocky Mountains. By Washington Irving. Chi. & N. Y. n. d., p. 100

previously, formed themselves into a company, composed of twelve partners, with a capital of about forty thousand dollars, called the Missouri Fur Company; the object of which was, to establish posts along the upper part of the river, and monopolize the trade.   The leading partner of this Company was Mr. Manual Lisa, a Spaniard by birth, and a man of bold and enterprising character, who had ascended the Missouri almost to its source, and made himself well acquainted and popular with several of its tribes.   By his exertions, trading posts had been established, in 1808, in the Sioux country, and among the Aricara and Mandan tribes; and a principal one, under Mr. Henry, one of the partners, at the forks of the Missouri.   This Company had in its employ about two hundred and fifty men, partly American hunters, and partly Creoles and Canadian voyageurs.

"All these circumstances combined to produce a population at St. Louis even more motley than that at Mackinaw. Here were to be seen, about the river banks, the hectoring, extravagant, bragging boatmen of the Mississippi, with the gay, grimacing, singing, good-humored Canadian voyageurs. Vagrant Indians, of various tribes, loitered about the streets. Now and then a stark Kentucky hunter, in leather hunting-dress, with a rifle on shoulder and knife in belt, strode along. Here and there were new brick houses and shops, just set up by bustling, driving and eager men of traffic from the Atlantic States; while, on the other hand, the old French mansions, with open casements, still retained the easy, indolent air of the original colonists; and now and then the scraping of a fiddle, a strain of an ancient French song, or the sound of billiard balls, showed that the happy Gallic turn for gayety and amusement still lingered about the place.

"Such was the St. Louis at the time of Mr. Hunt's arrival there, and the appearance of a new fur company, with ample funds at its command, produced a strong sensation among the Indian traders of the place, and awakened keen jealousy and opposition on the part of the Missouri Company.   Mr. Hunt proceeded to strengthen himself against all competition.   For this purpose, he secured to the interests of the Association another of those enterprising men, who had been engaged in individual traffic with the tribes of the Missouri. This was a Mr. Joseph Miller, a gentleman well educated and well informed, and of a respectable family of Baltimore. He had been an officer in the army of the United States, but had resigned in disgust, on being refused a furlough, and had taken to trapping beaver and trading among the Indians. He was easily induced by Mr. Hunt to join as a partner, and was considered by him, on account of his education and acquirements, and his experience in Indian trade, a valuable addition to the Company. Other arrangements were made for a quick departure, and forming a winter camp as far up the river as they could go that fall.

"Accordingly, on the twenty-first of October he took his departure from St. Louis. His party was distributed in three boats. One was the barge which he had brought from Mackinaw; another was of a larger size, such as was formerly used in navigating the Mohawk river, and known by the generic name of the Schenectody barge; the other was a large keel boat, at that time the grand conveyance on the Mississippi.

"In this way they set out from St. Louis, in buoyant spirits, and soon arrived at the mouth of the Missouri. This vast river, three thousand miles in length, and which, with its tributary streams, drains such an immense extent of country, was as yet but casually and imperfectly navigated by the adventurous bark of the fur trader, a steamboat had never yet stemmed its turbulent current. Sails were but of casual assistance, for it required a strong wind to conquer the force of the stream. The main dependence was on bodily strength and manual dexterity. The boats, in general, had to be propelled by oars and setting poles, or drawn by the hand and grappling hooks from one root or overhanging tree to another; or towed by the long cordelle, or towing line, where the shores were sufficiently clear of woods and thickets to permit the men to pass along the banks.

"During this slow and tedious progress, the boat would be exposed to frequent danger from floating trees and great masses of drifwood, or to be impaled upon snags and sawyers; that is to say, sunken trees, presenting a jagged or pointed end above the surface of the water. As the channel of the river frequently shifted from side to side, according to the bends and sand banks, the boat had, in the same way, to advance in a zigzag course. Often a part of the crew would have to leap into the water at the shallows, and wade along with the towing line, while their companions on board toilfully assisted with oar and setting pole. Sometimes the boat would seem to be retained motionless, as if spell-bound, opposite some point round which the current set with violence, and where the utmost labor scarce effected any visible progress.

"On these occasions it was that the merits of the Canadian voyageurs came into full action. Patient of toil, not to be disheartened by impediments and disappointments, fertile in expedients, and versed in every mode of humoring and conquering the wayward current, they would ply every exertion, sometimes in the boat, sometimes on shore, sometimes in the water, however cold; always alert, always in good humor; and should they at any time flag or grow weary, one of their popular boat songs, chanted by a veteran oarsman, and responded to in chorus, acted as a never-failing restorative.

"By such assiduous and persevering labor they made their way about four hundred and fifty miles up the Missouri, by the 16th of November, to the mouth of the Nodowa (2) as this was a good hunting country, and as the season was rapidly advancing, they determined to establish their winter quarters at this place; and, in fact two days after they had come to a halt, the river closed just above their encampment."

Here the party was joined by Mr. Robert McLellan a man who had distinguished himself in the Indian wars under General Wayne; also by John Day, a Virginian, who had for some years been in the employ of western traders. The

---

2. This was the present Nodaway river. In Bradbury's work it is called Naduet.

country around the place of encampment abounded in deer and wild turkeys, and provisions were abundant. From this place Mr. Hunt returned to St. Louis, to obtain an interpreter, acquainted with the language of the Sioux, and also additional hunters. He started on foot January 11, 1810; at Fort Osage, one hundred and fifty miles below, he bought two horses, and with two men, proceeded to St. Louis, where he arrived January 20th. Of his work then the author says:

"The greatest difficulty was to procure the Sioux interpreter. There was but one man to be met with at St. Louis who was fitted for the purpose, but to secure him would require much management. The individual in question was a half-breed, named Pierre Dorion; and as he figures hereafter in this narrative, and is, withal, a striking specimen of the hybrid race on the frontier, we shall give a few particulars concerning him. Pierre was the son of Dorion, the French interpreter, who accompanied Messrs. Lewis and Clarke in their famous exploring expedition across the Rocky mountains, old Dorion was one of those French creoles, descendants of the ancient Canadian stock, who abound on the western frontier, and amalgamate or cohabit with the savages. He had sojourned among various tribes, and perhaps left progeny among them all; but his regular or habitual wife was a Sioux squaw. By her he had a hopeful brood of half-breed sons, of whom Pierre was one. The domestic affairs of old Dorion were conducted on the true Indian plan. Father and sons would occasionally get drunk together, and then the cabin was a scene of ruffian brawl and fighting, in the course of which the old Frenchman was apt to get soundly belabored by his mongrel offspring. In a furious scuffle of the kind, one of the sons got the old man upon the ground, and was on the point of scalping him. "Hold! my son," cried the old fellow, in imploring accents, "you are too brave, too honorable to scalp your father!" This last appeal touched the French side of the half-breed's heart so he suffered the old man to wear his scalp unharmed.

*   *   *   *

"The moment it was discovered by Mr. Lisa that Pierre Dorion was in treaty with the new and rival association, he endeavored by threats as well as by promises, to prevent his engaging in their service.   His promises might, perhaps, have prevailed; but his threats, which related to the whiskey debt. only served to drive Pierre into the opposite ranks.   Still, he took advantage of this competition for his services to stand out Mr. Hunt on the most advantageous terms, and, after a negotiation of nearly two weeks, capitulated to serve in the expedition, as hunter and interpreter, at the rate of three hundred dollars a year, two hundred of which were to be paid in advance.

"When Mr. Hunt had got everything ready for leaving St. Louis new difficulties arose. * * * Even Pierre Dorion, at the last moment, refused to enter the boat until Mr. Hunt consented to take his squaw and two children on board also. * * *

"Among the various persons who were to proceed up the Missouri with Mr. Hunt, were two scientific gentlemen: one Mr. John Bradbury, (3) a man of mature age, but great enterprise and personal activity, who had been sent out by the Linnaean Society of Liverpool, to make a collection of American plants; the other, a Mr. Nuttall, likewise an Englishman, younger in years, who has since made himself known as the author of "Travels in Arkansas," and a work on the "Genera of American Plants." Mr. Hunt had offered them the protection and facilities of his party, in their scientific researches up the Missouri.   As they were not ready to depart at the moment of embarkation, they put their trunks on board of the boat, but remained at St. Louis until the next day, for the arrival of the post intending to join the expedition at St. Charles, a short distance above the mouth of the Missouri.

---

3.   Bradbury published an account of this expedition in "Travels in the Interior of America, in the years 1809, 1810, and 1811; including a description of Upper Louisiana, together with the States of Ohio, Kentucky, Indiana and Tennessee, with the Illinois and western territories. and containing remarks and observations useful to persons emigrating to these countries.   Liverpool; 1817."

"The same evening, however, they learned that a writ had
been issued against Pierre Dorion for his whiskey debt. by Mr.
Lisa, as agent of the Missouri Company, and that it was the
ntention to entrap the mongrel linguist on his arrival at St.
Charles. Upon hearing this, Mr. Bradbury and Mr. Nuttall
set off a little after midnight, by land, got ahead of the boat as
t was ascending the Missouri, before its arrival at St. Charles,
and gave Pierre Dorion warning of the legal toil prepared to
ensnare him. The knowing Pierre immediately landed and
took to the woods, followed by his squaw laden with their
papooses, and a large bundle contáining their most precious ef-
'ects, promising to rejoin the party some distance above St.
Charles. There seemed little dependence to be placed upon
promises of a loose adventurer of the kind, who was at the
very time playing an evasive game with his former employers;
who had already received two-thirds of his year's pay, and had
his rifle on his shoulder, his family and worldly fortune at his
heels, and the wild woods before him. There was no alterna-
tive, however, and it was hoped his pique against his old employers would render him faithful to his new ones.

"The party reached St. Charles in the afternoon, but the
harpies of the law looked in vain for their expected prey.
The boats resumed their course on the following morning, and
had not proceeded far when Pierre Dorion made his appearance
on shore. He was gladly taken on board, but he came without
his squaw. They had quarrelled in the night; Pierre had ad-
ministered the Indian discipline of the cudgel, whereupon she
had taken to the woods, with their children and all their
worldly goods. Pierre evidently was deeply grieved and dis-
concerted at the loss of his wife and his knapsack, wherefore
Mr. Hunt dispatched one of the Canadian voyageurs in search
of the fugitives; and the whole party, after proceeding a few
miles further, encamped on an island to await his return. The
Canadian rejoined the party, but without the squaw; and
Pierre Dorion passed a solitary and anxious night, bitterly re-
gretting his indiscretion in having exercised his conjugal au-
thority so near home. Before daybreak, however, a well-

known voice reached his ears from the opposite shore.   It
was his repentant spouse, who had been wandering the woods
all night in quest of the party, and had at length descried it
by its fires.   A boat was dispatched for her, the interesting
family was once more united, and Mr. Hunt now flattered himself that his perplexities with Pierre Dorion were at an end.

*   .   *   *   *

"On the afternoon of the third day, January 17th, the
boats touched at Charette, one of the old villages founded by
the original French colonists.   Here they met Daniel Boone,
the renowned patriarch of Kentucky, who had kept in the advance of civilization, and on the borders of the wilderness, still
leading a hunter's life, though now in his eighty-fifth year.
He had but recently returned from a hunting and trapping
expedition, and had brought nearly sixty beaver skins as
trophies of his skill.   The old man was still erect in form,
strong in limb, and unflinching in spirit, and as he stood on the
river bank, watching the departure of an expedition destined
to traverse the wilderness to the very shores of the Pacific. / ry
probably felt a throb of his old pioneer spirit, impelling him
to shoulder his rifle and join the adventurous band.   Boone
flourished several years after this meeting, in a vigorous old
age, the Nestor of hunters and backwoodsmen; and died, full
of sylvan honor and renown, in 1818, in his ninety-second
year. (4)

"The next morning early, as the party were yet encamped
at the mouth of a small stream, they were visited by another of
those heroes of the wilderness, one John Colter, who had accompanied Lewis and Clark in their memorable expedition. He
had recently made one of those vast internal voyages so char-

---

4.   There are conflicting statements about the birth and death of
Daniel Boone.   The Missouri volume of the U. S. Biographical Dictionary, Ellis' Life of Boone, Hill's Life of Boone, and Bryan's Life as
published in the Missouri Historical Review all give the date of his
death as September 26, 1820, and the above date, and that given in
Flint's Life of Boone is not correct.   Flint gives the date of his birth
as 1736; the Ellis and Hill, Feb. 11, 1735, the U. S. Biog. Dictionary,
Oct. 22, 1734, and Bryan August 22, 1834. The last we take to be
the correct date.

acteristic of this fearless class of men, and of the immense
regions over which they hold their lonely wanderings; having
come from the head-waters of the Missouri to St. Louis in a
small canoe.

* * * *

"Continuing their progress up the Missouri, the party
encamped, on the evening of the 21st of March, in the neighborhood of a little frontier village of French creoles.   Here
Pierre Dorion met with some of his old comrades, with whom
he had a long gossip, and returned to the camp with rumors of
bloody feuds between the Osages and the Ioways, or Ayaways,
Potowatomies, Sioux, and Sawkees.   Blood had already been
shed, and scalps been taken.   A war party, three hundred
strong, were prowling in the neighborhood, others might be
met with higher up the river; it behooved the travellers, there-
fore, to be upon their guard against robbery or surprise, for an
Indian war party on the march is prone to acts of outrage.

"In consequence of this report, which was subsequently
confirmed by further intelligence, a guard was kept up at
night around the encampment, and they all slept on their
arms.   As they were sixteen in number, and well supplied with
weapons and ammunition, they trusted to be able to give any
marauding party a warm reception.   Nothing occurred, however, to molest them on their voyage, and on the 8th of April,
they came in sight of Fort Osage.   On their approach the flag
was hoisted on the fort, and they saluted it by a discharge of
firearms.   Within a short distance of the fort was an Osage
village, the inhabitants of which, men, women and children,
thronged down to the water side to witness their landing.   One
of the first persons they met on the river bank was Mr. Crooks,
who had been down in a boat, with nine men, from the winter
encampment at Nodowa, to meet them.

"They remained at Ft. Osage a part of three days, during which they were hospitably entertained at the garrison by
Lieutenant Brownson, who held a temporary command.   They
were regaled also with a war-feast at the village; the Osage
warriors having returned from a successful forage against the

Ioways, in which they had taken seven scalps.　These were
paraded on poles about the village, followed by the warriors
decked out in all their savage ornaments, and hideously paint-
ed as if for battle.

"By the Osage warriors, Mr. Hunt and his companions
were again warned to be on their guard in ascending the
river, as the Sioux tribe meant to lay in wait and attack them.

"On the 10th of April they again embarked, their party
being now augmented to twenty-six, by the addition of Mr.
Crooks and his boat's crew.　They had not proceeded far,
however, when there was a great outcry from one of the
boats; it was occasioned by a little domestic discipline in the
Dorion family.　The squaw of the worthy interpreter, it ap-
peared, had been so delighted with the scalp-dance, and other
festivities of the Osage village, that she had taken a strong
inclination to remain there.　This had been as strongly op-
posed by her liege lord, who had compelled her to embark.
The good dame had remained sulky ever since, whereupon
Pierre seeing no other mode of exorcising the evil spirit out
of her, and being, perhaps, a little inspired by whiskey, had
resorted to the Indian remedy of the cudgel, and, before his
neighbors could interfere, had belabored her so soundly that
there is no record of her having shown any refractory symp-
toms throughout the remainder of the expedition.

"For a week they continued their voyage, exposed to
almost incessant rains.　The bodies of drowned buffaloes
floated past them in vast numbers; many had drifted upon
the shore or against the upper ends of rafts and islands.
These had attracted great flights of turkey-buzzards; some
were banqueting on the carcasses, others were soaring far
aloft in the sky, and others were perched on the trees, with
their backs to the sun, and their wings stretched out to dry,
like so many vessels in harbors, spreading their sails after
a shower.

"The turkey-buzzard (vulture aura, or golden vulture),
when on the wing, is one of the most specious and imposing
of birds.　Its flight in the upper regions of the air is really

sublime, extending its immense wings, and wheeling slowly and majestically to and fro seemingly without exerting a muscle or fluttering a feather, but moving by mere volition, and sailing on the bosom of the air as a ship upon the ocean. Usurping the empyreal realm of the eagle, he assumes for a time the post and dignity of that majestic bird, and often is mistaken for him by ignorant crawlers upon earth. It is only when he descends from the clouds to pounce upon carrion that he betrays his low propensities, and reveals his caitiff character Near at hand he is a disgusting bird, ragged in plumage, base in aspect, and of loathsome odor.

"On the 17th of April Mr. Hunt arrived with his party at the station near the Nodowa River, where the main body had been quartered during the winter.

"The weather continued rainy and ungenial for some days after Mr. Hunt's return to Nodowa; yet spring was rapidly advancing and vegetation was putting forth with all its early freshness and beauty. The snakes began to recover from their torpor and crawl forth into day, and the neighborhood of the wintering house seems to have been much infested with them. Mr. Bradbury, in the course of his botanical researches, found a surprising number in a half torpid state, under flat stones upon the banks which overhung the cantonment, and narrowly escaped being struck by a rattle-snake, which started at him from a cleft in the rock, but fortunately gave him warning by its rattle.

"The pigeons too were filling the woods in vast migratory flocks. It is almost incredible to describe the prodigious flights of these birds in the western wildernesses. They appear absolutely in clouds, and move with astonishing velocity. their wings making a whistling sound as they fly. The rapid evolutions of these flocks, wheeling and shifting suddenly a: if with one mind and one impulse; the flashing changes of color they present, as their backs, their breasts, or the under part of their wings are turned to the spectator, are singularly pleasing. When they alight, if on the ground, they cove: whole acres at a time; if upon trees, the branches often break be-

neath their weight. If suddenly startled while feeding in
the midst of a forest, the noise they make in getting on the
wing is like the roar of a cataract or the sound of distant
thunder.

"A flight of this kind, like an Egyptian flight of locusts,
devours everything that serves for its food as it passes along.
So great were the numbers in the vicinity of the camp that
Mr. Bradbury, in the course of a morning's excursion, shot
nearly three hundred with a fowling-piece. He gives a cu-
rious, though apparently a faithful, account of the kind of
discipline observed in these immense flocks, so that each may
have a chance of picking up food. As the front ranks must
meet with the greatest abundance, and the rear ranks must
have scanty picking, the instant a rank finds itself the hind-
most it rises in the air, flies over the whole flock, and takes
its place in the advance. The next rank follows in its course,
and thus the last is continually becoming first, and all by
turns have a front place at the banquet.

"The rains having at length subsided, Mr. Hunt broke
up the encampment and resumed his course up the Missouri.

"The party now consisted of nearly sixty persons; of
whom five were partners; one, John Reed, was a clerk; forty
were Canadian "voyageuers," of "engages," and there were
several hunters. They embarked in four boats, one of which
was of a large size, mounting a swivel and two howitzers. All
were furnished with masts and sails, to be used when the wind
was sufficently favorable and strong to overpower the current
of the river. Such was the case for the first four or five days,
when they were wafted steadily up the stream by a strong
southeaster.

"Their encampments at night were often pleasant and
picturesque; on some beautiful bank beneath spreading trees,
which afforded them shelter and fuel. The tents were pitched,
the fires made and the meals prepared by the voyageurs, and
many a story was told, and joke passed, and song sung, round
the evening fire. All, however, were asleep at an early hour.
Some under the tents, others wrapped in blankets before the

fire, or beneath the trees; and some few in the boats and canoes.

"On the 28th they breakfasted on one of the islands which lie at the mouth of the Nebraska or Platte river, the largest tributary of the Missouri, and about six hundred miles above its confluence with the Mississippi. * * * *

They were now beyond the limits of the present state of Missouri. and we leave them to pursue their course to the Pacific coast.

At a later date, Washington Irving made a trip through Missouri, and the **Missouri Intelligencer and Boon's Lick Advertiser** had the following notice of him: (5) "Washington Irving. This gentleman arrived in Columbia on Wednesday the 19th inst. and remained here until the next day, when he resumed his journey for the Osage country. From the notice in one of the St. Louis papers, announcing his arrival there. that he was on his way to the Upper Mississippi, we did not anticipate the honor of seeing him here. His destination, however, for the present at least, is different. He expressed the greatest surprise and admiration of what he had already seen of Missouri—having previously formed different views of the country. In his manners, Mr. Irving is unostentatious, affable and gentlemanly. He will no doubt acquire a valuable fund of materials in his progress, for interesting works or sketches, which, ere long, we may have the gratification of perusing."

The fullest account of this trip given by him is in a letter to a friend in Europe, which was published in the London Athenaeum, reprinted in the New York Commercial Advertiser, and copied in the Missouri Intelligencer and Boon's Lick Advertiser, and from the files of this paper in the library of the State Historical Society of Missouri we copy the letter, (6) which was not included in the "Life and Letters of Washington Irving by his nephew Pierre M. Irving:"

"Washington City, Dec. 18, 1832. I arrived here a few days since, from a tour of several months, which carried me

---

5. Sept. 29, 1832.
6. May 11, 1833.

far to the west, beyond the bounds of civilization.

"After I wrote to you in August, from I think Niagara, I proceeded with my agreeable fellow travelers, Mr. L. and Mr. P. (7) to Buffalo, and we embarked at Black Rock on Lake Erie. On board of the steamboat was Mr. E. one of the commissioners appointed by the government to superintend the settlement of the emigrant Indian tribes to the west of the Mississippi. He was on his way to the place of rendezvous, and on his invitation, we agreed to accompany him in his expedition. The offer was too tempting to be resisted. I should have an opportunity of seeing the remnants of those great Indian tribes which are now about to disappear as independent nations, or to be amalgamated under some new form of government. I should see those fine countries of the "far west," while still in a state of pristine wilderness, and behold herds of buffaloes scouring their native prairies, before they are driven beyond the reach of a civilized tourist.

"We, accordingly, traversed the centre of Ohio, and embarked in a steamboat at Cincinnati for Louisville, in Kentucky. Thence we descended the Ohio river in another steamboat, and ascended the Mississippi to St. Louis. Our voyage was prolonged by repeatedly running aground, in consequence of the lowness of the waters, and, on the first occasion we were nearly wrecked and sent to the bottom, by encountering another steamboat coming with all the impetus of a high pressure engine, and a rapid current. Fortunately, we had time to sheer a little so as to receive the blow obliquely, which carried away part of a wheel, and all the upper works on one side of the boat.

"From St. Louis I went to Fort Jefferson, about nine miles distant, to see Black Hawk, the Indian warrior, and his fellow prisoners—a forlorn crew, emaciated and dejected—the redoubtable chieftain himself, a meagre old man upwards of seventy. He has, however, a fine head, a Roman style of face, and a prepossessing countenance.

7. Mr. Chas. Joseph Latrobe and Count de Pourtales, the former of whom published "The Rambler in North America," 2 vols., London, 1832, in which he gives a full account of this trip.

"At St. Louis we bought horses for ourselves, and a covered wagon for our baggage, tents, provisions, etc., and traveled by land to Independence, a small frontier hamlet of log houses, situated between two and three hundred miles up the Missouri, on the utmost verge of civilization. * * * *

"From Independence, we struck across the Indian country, along the line of Indian missions; and arrived, on the 8th of October, after ten or eleven days' tramp, at Fort Gibson, a frontier town in Arkansas. Our journey lay almost entirely through vast prairies, or open grassy plains, diversified occassionally by beautiful groves, and deep fertile bottoms along the streams of water. We lived in frontier and almost Indian style, camping out at nights, except when we stopped at the missionaries, scattered here and there in this vast wilderness. The weather was serene, and we encountered but one rainy night and one thunder storm, and I found sleeping in a tent a very sweet and healthy repose. It was now upwards of three weeks since I had left St. Louis, and taken to traveling on horseback, and it agreed with me admirably.

"On arriving at Fort Gibson, we found that a mounted body of rangers nearly a hundred, had set off two days before to make a wide tour to the west and south through the wild hunting countries; by way of protecting the friendly Indians, who had gone to the buffalo hunting, and to overawe the Pawnees, who are the wandering Arabs of the west and are continually on the maraud. We determined to proceed on the track of this party, escorted by a dozen or fourteen horsemen (that we might have nothing to apprehend from any straggling party of Pawnees) and with three or four Indians as guides and interpreters, including a captive Pawnee woman. A couple of Creek Indians were despatched by the commander of the fort to overtake the party of rangers, and order them to to await our coming up with them. We were now to travel in still simple and rougher style, taking as little baggage as possible, and depending on our hunting for supplies; but were to go through a country abounding with game. The finest sport we had hitherto had was an incidental wolf hunt, as we were traversing a prairie, which was very animated and picturesque. I felt now completely launched in a savage life, and extremely excited and interested by this wild country, and the wild scenes and people by which I was surrounded. Our rangers were expert hunters, being mostly from Illinois, Tennessee, etc.

"We overtook the exploring party of mounted rangers in the course of three days, on the banks of the Arkansas; and the whole troop crossed that river on the 16th of October, some on rafts some fording. Our own immediate party had a couple of half breed Indians as servants, who understood the Indian customs. They constructed a kind of boat or raft, out of buffalo skin, on which Mr. E. and myself crossed the river and its branches, at several times, on the top of about a hundred weight of baggage—an odd mode of crossing a river a quarter of a mile wide.

"We now led a true hunting life, sleeping in the open air and living upon the produce of the chase, for we were three hundred miles beyond human habitation, and part of the time in a country hitherto unexplored.

" We got to the region of the buffaloes and wild horses; killed some of the former, and caught some of the latter. We were, moreover, on the hunting grounds of the Pawnees, the terror of that frontier; a race who scour the prairies on fleet horses, and are like the Tartars, or roving Arabs.

"We had to set guards round our camp, and tie up our horses for fear of surprise; but, though we had an occasional alarm, we passed through the country without seeing a single Pawnee. I brought off, however, the tongue of a buffalo, of my own shooting, as a trophy of my hunting, and am determined to rest my renown as a hunter upon that exploit, and never to descend to smaller game.

"We returned to Fort Gibson after a campaign of about thirty days, well seasoned by hunter's fare and hunter's life.

"From Ft. Gibson I was about five days descending the Arkansas to the Mississippi, in a steamboat a distance of

several hundred miles. I then continued down the latter river
to New Orleans, where I passed some days very pleasantly.

"New Orleans is one of the most motley and amusing
places in the United States; a mixture of America and Europe.
The French part of the city is a counterpart of some French
provincial town, and the levee or esplanade, along the river,
presents the most whimsical groups of people, of all nations,
casts and colors, French, Spanish, Indians, half-breeds, creoles,
mulattoes, Kentuckians, etc. I passed two days with M. on
his sugar plantation, just at the time when they were making
sugar.

"From New Orleans I set off, on the mail stage, through
Mobile, and proceeded on, through Alabama, Georgia, South
and North Carolina, and Virginia, to Washington, a long and
rather dreary journey, traveling frequently day and night,
and much of the road through pine forests, in the winter
season.

"At Columbia, the capital of South Carolina, I passed a
day most cordially with our friend P. I dined also with G. H. (8)
whom I had known in New York, when a young man, and
who is a perfect gentleman, though somewhat a Hotspur in
politics. It is really lamentable to see so fine a set of gallant
fellows, as the leading Nullifiers are, so sadly in the wrong.
They have just cause of complaint, and have been hardly
dealt with, but they are putting themselves completely in the
wrong by the mode they take to redress themselves, as a Com-
mittee of Congress is now occupied in the formation of a bill
for the reduction of the tariff. I hope that such a bill may
be devised and carried as will satisfy the moderate part of
the Nullifiers. But I grieve to see so many elements of na-
tional prejudice, hostility and selfishness, stirring and fer-
menting, with activity and acrimony.

"I intended stopping but a few days at Washington, and
then proceeding to New York; but I doubt now whether I
shall not linger for some time. I am very pleasantly situated;
I have a sunny, cheery, cosey little apartment in the immedi-

---

8.   Governor Hamilton, probably.

ate neighborhood of Mr. ———, and take my meals at his house, and in fact make it my home. I have thus the advantage of a family circle, and that a delightful one, and the precious comfort of a little batchelor retreat and sanctum sanctorum, where I can be as lonely and independent as I please. Washington is an interesting place to see public characters, and this is an interesting crisis. Everybody, too, is so much occupied with his own or the public business, that, now that I have got through the formal visits, I can have the time pretty much to myself.

"As to the kind of pledge I gave, you are correct in your opinion. It was given in the warmth and excitement of the moment; was from my lips before I was aware of its unqualified extent, and is to be taken *cum grane salis.* It is absolutely my intention to make our country my home for the residue of my li'e, and the more I see of it, the more I am convinced that I can live here with more enjoyment than in Europe, but I shall certainly pay my friends in France and relations in England, a visit, in the course of another year or two, to pass joyously a season in holiday style.

"You have no idea how agreeably one can live in this country, especially one, like myself, who can change place at will, and meet friends at every turn. Politics also, which makes such a figure in the newspapers, do not enter so much as you imagine into private life—and I think there is a better one respecting them generally, in society, than there was formerly; in fact, the mode of living, the sources of quiet enjoyment, and the sphere of friendly and domestic pleasures, are improved and multiplied to a degree that would delightfully surprise you."

In the "Life and Letters of Washington Irving" there are three letters written to his sister, Mrs. Paris, from St. Louis, from Independence, and from Ft. Gibson, Ark. In the first one in addition to what he told of Black Hawk. in the letter quoted, he says "He has a small, well-formed head, with an aquiline nose, a good expression of eye; and a physician present, who is given to craniology, perceived the organ of benevolence strongly developed, though I believe the old chieftain stands accused of many cruelties. His brother-in-law, the prophet, is a strong, stout man and much younger. He is considered the most culpable agent in fomenting the late disturbance; though I find it extremely difficult, even when so near the seat of action, to get at the right story of these feuds between the white and the red men, and my sympathies go strongly with the latter." (9)

In the second letter he wrote: "We arrived at this place day before yesterday, after nine days' travel on horseback from St. Louis. Our journey has been a very interesting one, leading us across fine prairies and through noble forests, dotted here and there by farms and log houses, at which we found rough but wholesome and abundant fare, and very civil treatment. Many parts of these prairies of the Missouri are extremely beautiful, resembling cultivated countries, embellished with parks and groves, rather than the savage rudeness of the wilderness.

"Yesterday I was out on a deer-hunt, in the vicinity of this place, which led me through some scenery that only wanted a castle, or a gentleman's seat here and there interspersed, to have equalled some of the most celebrated park scenery of England.

"The fertility of all this western country is truly astonishing. The soil is like that of a garden, and the luxuriance and beauty of the forests exceed any that I have seen. We have gradually been advancing, however, toward rougher life, and we are now at a little straggling frontier village, that has only been five years in existence. From hence, in the course of a day or two, we take our departure southwardly, and shall bid adieu to civilization, and camp at night in our tents." (10)

In the third letter there is nothing in addition to the letter quoted.

9. Life and letters of Washington Irving, by his nephew, Pierre M. Irving. N. Y., 1895. Vol. II, p. 264.
10. Ibid, p. 266.

LIBRARY OF CONGRESS
0 014 572 796 0